Navigating AI Language

A Glossary Guide to Artificial Intelligence

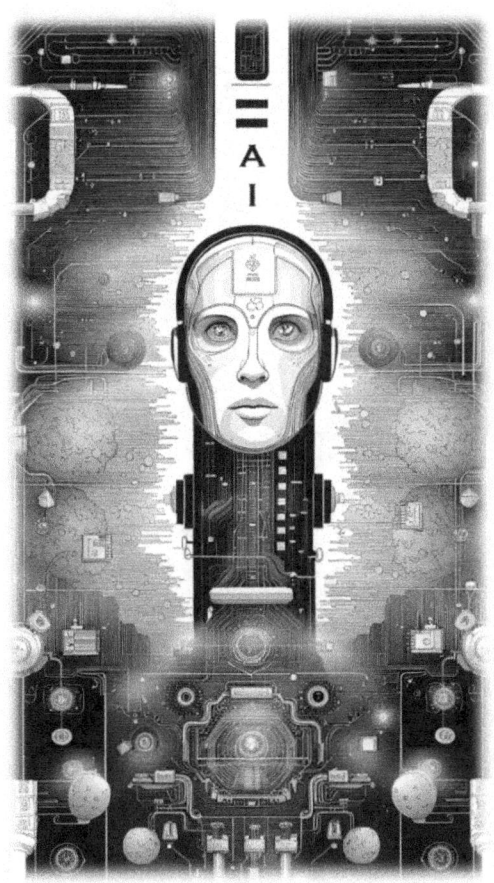

Dr. Joseph A. Ippolito

First Edition

ISBN: 9798861635707

Before We Begin

Dear Reader,

Artificial intelligence (AI) is a rapidly growing field that is transforming the way we work, interact, and understand the world. As you begin your journey in this fascinating field, it's important to be aware of the ever-evolving nature of AI. The terminology and definitions used to describe AI are constantly changing, and the pace of advancement is nothing short of remarkable.

Not long ago, AI was considered to be a niche concept, but it has quickly become a transformative force across industries. AI is used to power everything from self-driving cars to facial recognition software. This technology is changing the way we work, interact with each other, and understand the world around us.

The speed of advancement in AI is staggering. New breakthroughs are announced every day, and it can be difficult to keep up. As AI continues to evolve, so too will the terminology and definitions used to describe it. It's important to stay up-to-date on these changes in order to understand the latest developments in AI.

This book provides a thorough and current introduction to the terminology used in the field of artificial intelligence. However, it's important to remember that the AI field is constantly changing, with new concepts, technologies, and terms emerging all the time. This rapid evolution is a testament to the creativity and innovation of the AI community.

To use AI effectively, you need to stay up-to-date on the latest terms and technologies. This glossary is a good place to start, but it's just one resource. Here are a few tips for staying informed:

Stay Curious

Cultivate a curious mindset and a passion for learning. AI is a vast field with endless possibilities, so don't hesitate to explore new concepts and delve deeper into areas that intrigue you.

Follow Industry Trends

Keep an eye on industry news, research papers, and AI conferences. These sources are rich with insights into the latest developments and terminology in AI.

Engage with the Community

Join AI forums, online communities, and social media groups where professionals and enthusiasts share their knowledge and experiences. Engaging in discussions can provide valuable context to the terminology you encounter.

Lifelong Learning

Consider enrolling in online courses, attending workshops, or pursuing advanced degrees in AI-related disciplines. Lifelong learning is essential in a field as dynamic as AI.

Update Your Resources

Periodically revisit this glossary and other reference materials to ensure you are using the most current terminology and definitions.

The journey into artificial intelligence is an exciting and rewarding one, but it requires adaptability and a commitment to staying up-to-date on the latest developments. Embrace the changes, welcome the challenges, and keep an open mind to the infinite possibilities that AI offers.

With the right mindset and a commitment to lifelong learning, you'll not only be able to navigate the ever-changing AI landscape with confidence, but you'll also be able to contribute to its growth and innovation.

Happy exploring!

Sincerely,

J. Ippolito

Table of Contents

Before We Begin..**3**

Introduction 7

Artificial Intelligence (AI): A Brief History & Evolving Landscape 9

    Early Seeds of AI: Ancient Philosophical Musings................9

    The Mechanical Renaissance: Early Calculating Machines 10

    The Birth of Computing: Turing and the Turing Machine .10

    The Dartmouth Workshop: The Birth of AI as a Field 11

    The AI Winter and the Rise of Machine Learning 12

    The Internet Age: Big Data and the Deep Learning Revolution..13

    AI in Everyday Life: Virtual Assistants and Beyond 13

    AI Ethics and Bias: The Challenges Ahead.......................14

    The Future of AI: Challenges and Opportunities..............16

    Conclusion..16

Glossary of Terms **18**

Conclusion 104

Further Reading & Sources 105

Free AI Tools & Resources 109

Farewell 114

Introduction

Welcome to the world of Artificial Intelligence (AI)! It's an extremely fascinating and fast-changing field that has completely transformed the way we perceive and interact with technology. As we explore the intricacies of AI and its many applications, it becomes crucial to have a shared language that can facilitate understanding, communication, and collaboration among professionals, researchers, students, and enthusiasts.

This book primarily serves as a glossary and provides definitions for a wide range of terminologies, concepts, and methodologies that make up the realm of AI. Whether you're an academic engaged in deep research, a curious learner trying to grasp the fundamentals, or a practitioner staying updated with the latest advancements, this compilation offers a valuable resource to confidently navigate the ever-evolving AI landscape.

As artificial intelligence (AI) continues to shape industries, influence decision-making, and expand our capabilities, it is crucial to have a solid grasp of its foundational principles and nuanced terminology. This glossary provides a comprehensive overview of AI terminology, with definitions that bridge the gap between technical intricacies and accessible explanations. Additionally, the glossary covers terms from diverse AI subfields, including machine learning, deep learning, natural language processing, computer vision, robotics, ethics, and more.

This glossary is designed to be a valuable resource for anyone who wants to understand the rapidly evolving field of AI. It is an essential tool for researchers, developers, students, and anyone else who is interested in staying up-to-date on the latest AI trends.

As AI continues to shape our world, we invite you to explore, learn, and discover the terminology that propels us forward into an era of innovation, discovery, and boundless possibilities.

Note:

The rapid pace of AI development is characterized by breathtaking breakthroughs and innovations that seem to materialize overnight. As this field advances, new horizons are constantly explored, leading to the creation of novel concepts, methodologies, and technologies. Consequently, new terms emerge to capture these innovations, ensuring that the language of AI remains dynamic and ever-evolving. Just as AI itself learns and adapts, its lexicon evolves to accommodate the continuous expansion of its frontiers.

Be sure to visit the *Further Resources*
and *Free AI Tools* sections of this book!

Artificial Intelligence (AI):
A Brief History
& Evolving Landscape

Artificial Intelligence (AI) is a story of curiosity, innovation, and the relentless pursuit of a seemingly elusive goal: creating machines that can replicate human intelligence. While the modern era of AI research and development has produced remarkable advancements, its roots trace back to ancient myths, philosophical inquiries, and the emergence of computing machinery. This narrative spans centuries and reflects the enduring fascination with the idea of intelligent machines.

Early Seeds of AI: Ancient Philosophical Musings

The concept of intelligent, autonomous entities dates back to ancient civilizations. For example, Greek mythology featured automatons and intelligent machines created by Hephaestus, the god of blacksmiths and artisans. Philosophers such as Aristotle pondered the nature of thought and reasoning, laying the foundation for discussions on what it means to be intelligent.

During the 13th century, the prominent scholar Thomas Aquinas delved into the notion of artificial beings possessing intellect, thus paving the way for a multitude of philosophical deliberations spanning centuries regarding the interplay between humans and machines. The origins of artificial intelligence, even in its nascent stages, were firmly grounded in philosophical and metaphysical examinations that primarily centered around the essence of cognition and rationality.

The Mechanical Renaissance: Early Calculating Machines

The Renaissance period saw the development of mechanical devices designed to perform calculations. Blaise Pascal's Pascaline (1642) and Gottfried Wilhelm Leibniz's stepped reckoner (1673) were among the first mechanical calculators. These devices were not intelligent by modern standards, but they represented a critical step toward the automation of intellectual tasks.

The Birth of Computing: Turing and the Turing Machine

The emergence of modern computing in the 20th century marked a pivotal moment in the history of AI. The work of British mathematician and logician Alan Turing played a central role in this transformation. In 1936, Turing introduced the concept of a theoretical machine capable of performing any mathematical computation, now known as the Turing machine. This theoretical construct laid the foundation for the digital computer.

During World War II, Turing played a crucial role in breaking the German Enigma code, demonstrating the practical applications of computational machines. His ideas about machine intelligence and his famous Turing Test, introduced in his 1950 paper Computing Machinery and Intelligence, challenged the notion of what it means to be intelligent and set the stage for AI research.

The Dartmouth Workshop:
The Birth of AI as a Field

The concept of Artificial Intelligence was first introduced in 1956 during the organization of the *Dartmouth Workshop* by John McCarthy, Marvin Minsky, Nathaniel Rochester, and Claude Shannon. This landmark event served as the catalyst for the formalization of AI as a dedicated field of study. The participants of the workshop harbored high hopes regarding the prospect of developing intelligent machines, firmly believing that a computer program had the potential to accurately replicate a wide array of human intellectual activities.

Early AI Challenges:
Symbolic AI and Expert Systems

In the early days of artificial intelligence (AI) research, the predominant approach was symbolic AI. Researchers sought to represent knowledge and reasoning using symbols and logic. They developed expert systems, which were computer programs designed to mimic human expertise in specific domains. One of the most famous early expert systems was *Dendral*, developed in the 1960s to analyze chemical mass spectrometry data.

However, early AI systems faced significant limitations. They struggled with common-sense reasoning and lacked the ability to adapt and learn from experience. Symbolic AI's top-down approach of explicitly programming rules and knowledge proved inadequate for tackling complex, real-world problems.

The AI Winter and the Rise of Machine Learning

Despite initial enthusiasm, AI research encountered significant challenges in the 1970s and 1980s, leading to a period known as the "AI winter." Progress in AI was slower than expected, and funding decreased. This period witnessed the fading of symbolic AI and the emergence of machine learning as a dominant paradigm.

Machine learning, particularly the subfield of neural networks, experienced a resurgence in the 1980s and 1990s. Pioneering work by researchers such as Geoffrey Hinton and Yann LeCun led to breakthroughs in artificial neural networks. Their research paved the way for practical applications of machine learning, including speech recognition and computer vision.

The Internet Age:
Big Data and the Deep Learning Revolution

The turn of the 21st century ushered in a new era for AI, driven by the proliferation of digital data and the increasing power of computing. The availability of vast datasets, combined with advancements in graphics processing units (GPUs), enabled the training of deep neural networks.

Deep learning, a subset of machine learning, became a game-changer. Deep neural networks, inspired by the structure of the human brain, demonstrated remarkable performance in image and speech recognition, natural language processing, and reinforcement learning. In 2012, AlexNet, a deep convolutional neural network, won the ImageNet competition, marking a pivotal moment in computer vision.

AI in Everyday Life:
Virtual Assistants and Beyond

The proliferation of artificial intelligence in our day-to-day lives has gained momentum alongside the emergence of virtual assistants such as Apple's Siri, Amazon's Alexa, and Google Assistant. These sophisticated applications have effectively showcased the viability of speech recognition, natural language comprehension, and task automation. Consequently, individuals have gradually developed a consistent interaction with AI systems, heavily relying on them for accessing information, setting reminders, and enjoying recreational content.

AI Ethics and Bias:
The Challenges Ahead

As AI systems became more integrated into society, ethical concerns and questions of bias gained prominence. Issues related to privacy, fairness, transparency, and accountability in AI decision-making processes sparked debates and calls for responsible AI development.

The rising complexity and enhanced capabilities of AI systems have raised apprehensions about the potential introduction of bias and discrimination into their decision-making processes. This is because AI systems are often trained on data sets that reflect the biases of the human world, and these biases can be unintentionally encoded into the algorithms that power these systems. As a result, AI systems can perpetuate discriminatory practices and make decisions that are unfair or harmful to certain groups of people.

For example, a study by the AI Now Institute found that facial recognition software is more likely to misidentify people of color than Caucasians. This is because the software was trained on data sets that were predominantly white, and as a result, it has learned to associate certain features with being non-white. This can lead to serious problems, such as people being denied access to services or being arrested or detained because they are misidentified by a facial recognition system.

In addition to the concerns about AI bias discussed above, there are also concerns about the potential for these systems to be used for surveillance and to invade people's privacy. AI systems can be used to track people's movements, monitor their online activity, and even listen to their conversations. This can have a chilling effect on free speech and expression, and it can also lead to people being targeted for discrimination or persecution.

In order to address these concerns, it is essential to develop AI systems that are fair, transparent, and accountable. This means that AI systems should not be biased against certain groups of people, and they should be able to explain why they are making the decisions they make. It also means that there should be clear rules and regulations governing the use of AI systems, and that there should be mechanisms for people to challenge decisions made by AI systems.

The development of responsible AI is a complex and challenging task, but it is essential if we want to ensure that AI systems are used for good and not for harm. By addressing the ethical concerns and questions of bias that surround AI, we can help to create a more just and equitable world.

The Future of AI:
Challenges and Opportunities

The field of artificial intelligence (AI) has a rich history that is characterized by significant breakthroughs, setbacks, and paradigm shifts. Presently, AI is progressing *rapidly* and finds applications in various domains such as autonomous vehicles, healthcare diagnostics, financial forecasting, and creative content generation.

Looking ahead, there are several challenges that need to be addressed. These include tackling the ethical and societal implications of AI, ensuring responsible deployment of AI systems, and leveraging AI to bring benefits to humanity. The future holds great promise for AI, with endeavors to achieve artificial general intelligence (AGI) and exploring the potential of quantum computing in AI applications.

Given the dynamic nature of this field, it is crucial for researchers, policymakers, industry leaders, and society as a whole to collaborate. This collaboration will play a vital role in effectively navigating the evolving AI frontier and unlocking its immense potential.

Conclusion

The narrative of Artificial Intelligence's history is one imbued with human creativity, determination, and an unwavering commitment to the creation of machines

16

capable of thinking, learning, and adapting. Spanning from ancient myths and philosophical contemplations to the advent of modern computing and machine learning, AI's evolution has been remarkable. Its influence continues to shape our world, urging us to explore uncharted territories while also necessitating thoughtful consideration of the ethical and societal implications associated with intelligent machines.

Moving forward, the future of AI presents us with both challenges and opportunities. It is incumbent upon us to responsibly guide its development, guaranteeing that AI remains a catalyst for progress, comprehension, and groundbreaking innovation in the years that lie ahead.

Glossary of Terms

Abstract Syntax Tree (AST): Tree representation of source code syntax used in AI for code analysis and generation.

Activation Function: Nonlinear function applied to the output of individual neurons in neural networks.

Activation Map: A visual representation of the output of individual neurons or filters in a convolutional neural network (CNN), highlighting the regions of interest in an image.

Actor-Critic Method: Reinforcement learning technique combining value and policy estimation.

AdaBoost: Adaptive boosting AI algorithm that combines multiple weak classifiers to create a strong classifier.

Adaptive Learning: AI-driven educational technology that adjusts the pace and content of learning materials based on individual student performance and preferences.

Adversarial Attacks: Deliberate manipulation of AI models by adding imperceptible changes to input data to provoke incorrect outputs.

Adversarial Training: Improving model robustness by including adversarial examples during training.

Affective Computing: Enabling AI systems to recognize, interpret, process, and simulate human emotions.

Agglomerative Clustering: Bottom-up hierarchical clustering approach starting with individual points.

AI-driven Personalization: The use of AI algorithms to customize user experiences, such as content recommendations and product suggestions, based on individual preferences and behavior.

AI-enhanced Creativity: The use of AI tools and algorithms to augment and inspire human creativity in fields such as design, writing, and music composition.

AI Ethics: Principles safeguarding humans from AI harm, encompassing guidelines for data handling, bias mitigation, and fair decision-making.

AI Explainability: The ability to understand and interpret the decisions and predictions made by AI models, essential for transparency and trust.

AI Fairness: The concept of ensuring that AI systems do not discriminate against individuals or groups based on factors like race, gender, or age.

AI-Generated Art: Artwork, music, or other creative content generated or enhanced using artificial intelligence algorithms and models.

AI Governance: The development and implementation of policies and frameworks to regulate the responsible and ethical use of artificial intelligence.

AI Hardware Accelerator: Specialized hardware, such as GPUs (Graphics Processing Units) and TPUs (Tensor Processing Units), designed to accelerate AI model training and inference tasks.

AI in Healthcare: The application of AI techniques and technologies to improve diagnosis, treatment, and healthcare processes.

AI Marketplace: A platform or ecosystem where AI developers and users can buy, sell, or exchange AI algorithms, models, and services.

AI-powered Chatbots: Chatbot systems that use artificial intelligence to engage in natural language conversations, often used in customer support and virtual assistants.

AI-powered Virtual Reality (VR): The integration of artificial intelligence into virtual reality experiences to create more immersive and responsive VR environments.

AI Research Ethics: Guidelines and principles governing the ethical conduct of research involving artificial intelligence, particularly in experimental studies and data collection.

AI Safety: A multidisciplinary domain addressing potential adverse outcomes of AI, including sudden superintelligent behavior detrimental to humans.

Automatic Speech Recognition (ASR): The AI technology that converts spoken language into written text, used in applications like voice assistants and transcription services.

Autonomous Vehicles: Self-driving cars and trucks that use AI and sensor technology to navigate and make driving decisions without human intervention.

Algorithm: A sequence of instructions enabling computer programs to learn, process data, recognize patterns, and autonomously accomplish tasks.

Algorithmic Accountability: Ethical need for organizations to explain, justify, and take responsibility for algorithmic decision-making.

Algorithmic Bias: The presence of unfair or discriminatory outcomes in AI systems due to biased training data or flawed algorithms.

Algorithmic Fairness: Ensuring algorithmic systems produce equitable outcomes for different social groups.

Algorithmic Transparency: Principle that organizations should explain algorithms and enable examination of algorithmic decision-making.

Alignment: The process of refining AI to produce desired results, applicable to content moderation, enhancing human interactions, and more.

Ambient Intelligence: A form of AI that involves smart environments equipped with sensors and devices to enhance human experiences and automate tasks seamlessly.

Analog AI: AI systems that use analog components, such as analog neural networks, to perform computations in a manner more akin to biological brains.

Anomaly Detection: AI task of identifying rare or unusual instances in data that deviate from the norm.

Anthropomorphism: The tendency to attribute human-like qualities to non-human entities, including perceiving AI chatbots as sentient or emotional.

Artificial General Intelligence (AGI): An advanced form of AI surpassing contemporary capabilities, excelling in tasks beyond human capacity, while also fostering self-improvement.

Artificial Intelligence (AI): Technology simulating human intellect, encompassing computer programs and robotics, designed to perform human-like tasks.

Attention Mechanism: Component of neural networks that learns to focus on relevant parts of input data.

Artificial Neural Network (ANN): A computational model inspired by the structure and function of the human brain, consisting of interconnected nodes (neurons) used in machine learning.

Augmented Reality (AR): Technology blending digital elements with the real world, often in visual form, enhancing user experiences.

Autoencoder: A neural network architecture designed for data compression and reconstruction tasks.

Automated Machine Learning (AutoML): Automating the end-to-end process of applying machine learning.

B

Backpropagation: AI algorithm used in training neural networks by adjusting model weights based on error gradients.

Backward Chaining: An inference technique in AI where reasoning starts with a goal and works backward through a set of rules to determine if it can be satisfied.

Bag of Words (BoW): A text analysis technique in natural language processing (NLP) that represents text as a collection of individual words, ignoring grammar and word order.

Bagging: Ensemble method using bootstrap sampling to train base models on different data subsets.

Batch Learning: A machine learning approach where models are trained on a fixed dataset, as opposed to online learning where models continuously adapt to new data.

Bayesian Networks: Graphical models representing probabilistic relationships among variables.

Bayesian Optimization: Optimization technique using probabilistic models to efficiently search for optimal hyperparameters.

Beam Search: Efficient search algorithm retaining a fixed number of promising solutions at each step.

Behavior Cloning: A machine learning technique where an AI model is trained to mimic human behavior by learning from demonstration.

Behavioral Analytics: The use of AI and data analysis to track and understand user behavior, often applied in marketing, security, and user experience optimization.

Behavior-based Segmentation: An AI-driven marketing strategy that categorizes customers based on their online behavior and interactions, allowing for personalized marketing campaigns.

BERT (Bidirectional Encoder Representations from Transformers): A pre-trained natural language processing model that uses bidirectional context to improve the understanding of words in sentences, widely used in NLP tasks.

Bias Amplification: Phenomenon where biased AI models can exacerbate existing prejudices or disparities present in training data.

Bias Mitigation: Strategies to reduce biases in AI models and ensure equitable outcomes.

Bias: Errors arising from training data leading to incorrect attribution of characteristics to groups, often tied to stereotypes in large language models.

Bias-Variance Tradeoff: A fundamental concept in machine learning where model bias and variance are balanced to achieve optimal predictive performance.

Big Data: Extremely large and complex data sets that require advanced AI and computational techniques for analysis and insights.

Binary Classification: A type of machine learning task in which the model categorizes input data into one of two possible classes or categories.

Biological Neural Networks: The networks of neurons in the human brain that have inspired the architecture of artificial neural networks in AI.

Biometric Authentication: The use of AI and biometric data, such as fingerprints, facial recognition, or iris scans, to verify a person's identity.

Black Box Model: AI model whose internal workings are not transparent or easily interpretable.

Blockchain and AI: The integration of artificial intelligence and blockchain technology to enhance security, transparency, and trust in various applications.

Blockchain Smart Contracts: Self-executing contracts with the terms directly written into code on a blockchain, often used with AI for automation and trust in business transactions.

Bootstrapping: A resampling technique in machine learning that generates multiple subsets of the training data to improve model robustness and accuracy.

Botnet Detection: The use of AI algorithms to identify and mitigate botnets, networks of compromised computers used for malicious activities.

Bots and AI Chatbots: Programs that use artificial intelligence to automate tasks or engage in conversations with users, commonly used in customer support and online interactions.

Brain-Computer Interface (BCI): Technology that enables direct communication between the brain and external devices, often used in AI applications for healthcare and assistive technology.

Business Intelligence (BI): The use of AI and data analytics to extract valuable insights from organizational data to support decision-making.

Byzantine Fault Tolerance: A concept in distributed systems and AI where a network or system can function correctly even when some of its components (nodes) fail or behave maliciously.

C

Canonicalization: The process of converting data into a standard or canonical form, often applied in data preprocessing and cleaning in AI.

Capsule Network: An advanced neural network architecture designed to overcome limitations in traditional convolutional networks, particularly for image recognition tasks.

Capsule Networks: Neural networks using capsules to represent attributes of objects and their relationships.

Causal Inference: The process of determining cause-and-effect relationships from observational data, a critical concept in AI for understanding the impact of actions.

Chatbot: A program interacting with humans through text, mimicking human language and conversation.

ChatGPT: An AI language model developed by OpenAI, designed for natural language understanding and generation.

ChatOps: A collaboration model where AI chatbots are used to facilitate and automate DevOps tasks, improving communication and efficiency.

Class Activation Map (CAM): Technique producing heatmaps to visualize parts of images that AI models focus on.

Classification: AI task of assigning input data to predefined categories or classes.

Clickbait Detection: Identifying sensationalized headlines designed to attract clicks rather than convey accurate information.

Cloud AI: AI services and platforms delivered via the cloud, allowing organizations to access AI capabilities without the need for significant infrastructure.

Clustering: AI technique grouping similar data points together based on certain characteristics or features.

Cognitive Bias in AI: The presence of biases in AI models that may reflect or amplify societal biases, leading to unfair or discriminatory outcomes.

Cognitive Computing: A synonym for artificial intelligence, encompassing technology replicating cognitive functions.

Collaborative Filtering: An AI recommendation technique that makes predictions by leveraging the preferences and behavior of similar users.

Combinatorial Optimization: Finding optimal object from finite set of objects, useful for routing, scheduling, etc.

Commonsense Reasoning: The ability of AI systems to make inferences and decisions based on general knowledge and common sense, often used to enhance natural language understanding.

Computational Creativity: AI exhibiting creative behavior like humans including art, music, humor, storytelling.

Computer Vision: The field of AI focused on enabling computers to interpret and understand visual information from the world.

Concept Drift: The phenomenon in machine learning where the statistical properties of the data change over time, requiring models to adapt continuously.

Content Filtering: The use of AI algorithms to automatically classify and filter digital content, often used for content moderation and recommendation systems.

Contextual Bandits: A reinforcement learning framework where an AI agent makes decisions based on incomplete information.

Conversational AI: AI systems designed to engage in human-like conversations, including chatbots, virtual assistants, and customer service agents.

Convolutional Neural Network (CNN): A type of artificial neural network designed for processing grid-like data, such as images and videos, using convolutional layers to extract features.

Counterfactual Reasoning: A form of AI reasoning where the system considers alternative scenarios and outcomes, often used in decision-making and game theory.

Criticism Training: Improving dialog agents by exposing them to critiques from other agents during training.

Cross-Domain Transfer Learning: A technique in machine learning where knowledge gained from one domain or task is applied to another, often used to improve model performance with limited data.

Cross-Validation: A technique in machine learning used to assess the performance of a model by splitting the data into multiple subsets, training on some and testing on others to evaluate generalization.

Crowdsourcing: The practice of obtaining input, data, or labor from a large group of people, often used in AI for tasks like data labeling and validation.

Curiosity-driven Learning: An AI approach where models are incentivized to explore and learn from their environment, commonly used in reinforcement learning.

Curriculum Learning: A machine learning approach that gradually increases the complexity of training data to help models learn more effectively, often used in reinforcement learning.

Cybersecurity AI: The use of artificial intelligence to detect and respond to cybersecurity threats, such as malware and intrusions, in real-time.

D

Data Augmentation: The process of remixing existing or diverse data to train AI systems more effectively.

Data Democratization: Enabling broader access to data science and AI capabilities.

Data Fusion: The process of integrating data from multiple sources, such as sensors or databases, to provide a more comprehensive and accurate representation.

Data Imputation: Filling missing data points using AI techniques to maintain dataset completeness.

Data Labeling: The process of assigning tags or categories to data, often used to create labeled datasets for AI training.

Data Leakage: The unintentional inclusion of information from the test dataset in the training process, leading to overly optimistic model evaluations and potential biases.

Data Preprocessing: Cleaning, transforming, and organizing raw data before feeding it into AI models.

Decision Tree: AI model that represents decisions and their possible consequences in a tree-like structure.

Decision Trees: Hierarchical AI models used for classification and regression tasks, consisting of a tree-like structure.

Deep Learning: A subset of machine learning utilizing complex patterns recognition through artificial neural networks, inspired by the human brain.

Deep Reinforcement kindle Learning: An advanced form of machine learning where agents learn to make sequences of decisions in an environment to maximize cumulative rewards, often used in robotics and game playing.

Dialog System: AI-powered systems that engage in conversations with users, often used in virtual assistants, customer support, and chatbots.

Differential Privacy: A privacy-preserving mechanism in AI and data analysis that adds noise to data to protect individuals' information while still allowing for useful analysis.

Diffusion: A machine learning technique introducing random noise to existing data, with models trained to recover the original information.

Dimensionality Reduction: Techniques to reduce the number of features in data while preserving essential information.

Distributed AI: The deployment of AI models and algorithms across multiple devices or servers in a network, often used for edge computing and real-time processing.

Distributed Computing: The use of multiple computers or nodes to work together on a single problem or task, often used in AI for parallel processing and scalability.

Diversity in AI: The practice of ensuring varied and inclusive datasets and AI systems to prevent bias and promote fairness and representation.

Document Embedding: Techniques in natural language processing (NLP) to convert documents or text into continuous vector representations, facilitating analysis and similarity calculations.

Domain Adaptation: The process of modifying or fine-tuning an AI model trained in one domain to perform well in a different, but related, domain.

Dropout: Regularization technique in neural networks where random neurons are dropped out during training to prevent overfitting.

Dynamic Programming: An optimization technique in AI and algorithms where problems are solved by breaking them into smaller subproblems and storing their solutions to avoid redundant computations.

E

Edge Computing: A computing paradigm where AI processing is done on or near the data source or device, reducing latency and enabling real-time AI applications.

Emergent Behavior: Unintended AI capabilities that arise during operation.

End-to-End Learning (E2E): A deep learning approach where models learn tasks holistically from input to solution, rather than sequentially.

Ensemble Learning: Approach where multiple AI models are combined to improve prediction accuracy and robustness.

Ensemble Methods: Techniques in machine learning where multiple AI models, often of different types, are combined to improve overall prediction accuracy and robustness.

Ensemble Pruning: Eliminating redundant base models from ensembles to improve efficiency.

Entity Recognition: An AI and natural language processing (NLP) task that involves identifying and categorizing entities, such as names of people, places, or organizations, in text data.

Epoch: One complete iteration of AI model training using the entire dataset.

Ethical AI Design: Incorporating ethical considerations into AI model development to avoid harmful consequences.

Ethical Considerations: Awareness of ethical implications related to AI, including privacy, fairness, misuse, and safety.

Event Detection: An AI task that involves identifying and classifying events or patterns of interest in data streams, often used in applications like fraud detection and monitoring.

Evolutionary Algorithms: AI optimization methods inspired by biological evolution, involving selection and mutation processes.

Evolutionary Computation: A family of AI optimization algorithms, including genetic algorithms, evolutionary strategies, and genetic programming, inspired by biological evolution and natural selection.

Evolutionary Strategy: Black box optimization inspired by biological evolution mechanisms.

Exascale Computing: High-performance computing systems capable of performing one quintillion (10^{18}) calculations per second, enabling advanced AI simulations and analysis.

Expert System: AI software that emulates the decision-making abilities of a human expert in a particular domain by using knowledge-based rules and reasoning.

Explainability in AI: The degree to which an AI model's decisions and predictions can be understood and interpreted by humans, often essential for transparency and trust.

Explainable AI (XAI): AI models designed to provide transparent and understandable explanations for their decisions.

Explainable Reinforcement Learning: Enabling transparency in decisions made by RL agents.

F

Face Recognition: AI task of identifying and verifying individuals based on facial features.

Facial Landmarks: Distinct points on a face, such as the corners of the eyes or the tip of the nose, used in AI for tasks like facial recognition and emotion analysis.

Fairness in AI: The principle of ensuring that AI systems and algorithms do not discriminate against individuals or groups based on factors such as race, gender, or age.

False Positive: In AI and machine learning, it refers to a situation where a model incorrectly identifies something as positive (e.g., as an anomaly or a disease) when it is not.

Fault Tolerance: An attribute of AI systems that can continue to function correctly even in the presence of hardware or software failures.

Feature Engineering: Process of selecting, transforming, or creating input features to enhance AI model performance.

Feature Extraction: The process of automatically selecting or extracting relevant information or features from data for use in machine learning and AI algorithms.

Feature Selection: Process of choosing relevant input features to improve AI model performance and interpretability.

Federated AI: A variation of federated learning where AI models and algorithms are distributed and collaboratively trained across different organizations while preserving data privacy.

Federated Learning: Training AI models across decentralized devices while keeping data on the devices rather than centralizing it.

Feedback Loop: In AI, it refers to a mechanism where the output of a system influences its future behavior, often used in reinforcement learning and control systems.

Fine-grained Classification: A type of AI task that involves categorizing data into highly specific classes or categories, often used in image and object recognition.

Fine-tuning: The process of further training a pre-trained AI model on specific data or tasks to adapt it for particular applications or improve its performance.

Foom: The concept that the creation of AGI could lead to rapid, uncontrollable progress posing risks to humanity.

Forecasting: The use of AI and statistical methods to make predictions about future events or trends based on historical data.

Fuzzy Logic: A mathematical framework in AI and control systems that deals with uncertainty and imprecision, allowing for degrees of truth instead of binary true/false values.

G

Gaussian Distribution: Common AI probability distribution also known as the normal distribution.

Generative Adversarial Networks (GANs): AI models comprising a generator and discriminator network, collaborating to generate new data.

Generative AI: Technology using AI to create novel content like text, images, or code, relying on training data patterns.

Google Bard: A Google AI chatbot drawing on real-time internet data for responses, unlike ChatGPT, which uses data up to 2021.

Gradient Boosting: Ensemble learning method that builds models sequentially, each correcting the errors of the previous one.

Gradient Descent: Optimization algorithm used to minimize loss functions and train AI models.

Guardrails: Policies limiting AI behavior and content creation to ensure responsible usage.

Generalization: The ability of an AI model to make accurate predictions or decisions on new, unseen data that was not part of the training dataset.

GPU (Graphics Processing Unit): Hardware accelerators often used in AI and machine learning to speed up the training and inference of deep learning models.

Genome Sequencing: The process of determining the order of DNA nucleotides in an organism's genome, often aided by AI for analysis and interpretation.

Geospatial AI: The application of AI and machine learning techniques to analyze and derive insights from geospatial data, such as satellite imagery and location-based data.

Graph Database: A database system designed to store and manage data with complex relationships and structures, often used in AI applications that involve graph data.

Game AI: The field of AI that focuses on developing intelligent agents capable of playing and competing in video games, often used for non-player characters (NPCs) and opponent behavior.

Gesture Recognition: An AI technology that interprets and understands human gestures, often used in human-computer interaction and virtual reality systems.

Goal-Oriented AI: AI systems designed to achieve specific objectives or goals, often used in optimization problems and decision-making.

Geometric Deep Learning: A subfield of deep learning that extends neural networks to operate on structured and graph data, such as 3D shapes and networks.

GPU Accelerated Computing: The use of GPUs to accelerate various computational tasks, including AI model training and scientific simulations.

H

Hallucination: Incorrect AI responses, including generative AI producing confident but inaccurate answers.

Hard Example Mining: Selecting challenging examples during AI model training to improve robustness.

Hierarchical Clustering: AI technique that groups data points in a tree-like structure based on similarity.

Hyperparameter: Parameters set before AI model training that control its behavior and performance.

Hyperparameter Optimization: Process of finding optimal hyperparameter values to enhance AI model performance.

Hyperparameters: Variables defining AI model architecture and behavior, set before training.

Heteroscedasticity: In AI and statistics, it refers to the situation where the variance of the errors or residuals in a model is not constant across all levels of the independent variables.

Heuristic: A rule of thumb or problem-solving strategy that uses practical or domain-specific knowledge to make approximate decisions or find solutions, often used in AI algorithms.

Human-in-the-Loop (HITL): An AI system or process that involves human intervention or oversight to handle complex tasks, verify results, or improve system performance.

Hardware AI Accelerator: Specialized hardware, such as GPUs, TPUs, and AI-specific chips, designed to accelerate AI model training and inference.

Hybrid AI: An approach that combines different AI techniques or technologies, such as rule-based AI and machine learning, to solve complex problems.

Hypothesis Testing: A statistical procedure in AI and data analysis used to determine whether a hypothesis about a population parameter is supported by sample data.

Human-AI Collaboration: The interaction and cooperation between humans and AI systems to solve problems, make decisions, or achieve tasks more effectively.

Hypergraph: A generalization of a graph data structure that allows for edges to connect multiple nodes, often used in AI for representing complex relationships.

Homomorphic Encryption: A cryptographic technique used in AI and data privacy that allows computations to be performed on encrypted data without decrypting it, preserving privacy.

Human Pose Estimation: An AI computer vision task that involves detecting and estimating the position and orientation of human body parts in images or videos.

I

Image Inpainting: Reconstructing missing or corrupted parts of images using AI.

Imbalanced Dataset: A dataset where one class has significantly more samples than others, challenging AI training.

Imitation Learning: Learning to mimic expert behavior from demonstrations.

Imputation: Filling missing values in datasets using AI techniques to maintain data completeness.

Incremental Clustering: A clustering technique in AI that groups data incrementally as it arrives, rather than all at once, often used for real-time data streams.

Incremental Learning: A machine learning approach where an AI model is updated and improved continuously over time as new data becomes available, without retraining from scratch.

Independent Component Analysis: AI technique that separates a multivariate signal into additive components.

Individual Fairness: Similar individuals should be treated similarly by algorithmic systems.

Inductive Transfer: Transferring knowledge from one task to another different but related task.

Inference Attack: A security and privacy threat in AI and data analysis where an attacker can gain information about sensitive data or the model's behavior by making queries or observations.

Inference Engine: A component of an AI system that processes input data and uses a model or set of rules to make predictions, decisions, or classifications.

Inference: The process of using a trained AI model to make predictions or generate outputs based on new data.

Information Retrieval: AI field focused on finding relevant information from large datasets in response to user queries.

In-Memory Computing: A computing paradigm that stores and processes data primarily in RAM (random-access memory), often used for real-time AI applications.

In-Memory Database: A database system that stores and manages data primarily in RAM, often used in AI applications requiring fast data retrieval.

Instance: A single data point or example in a dataset, often used in the context of supervised learning, where instances have features and associated labels.

Interpolation: A mathematical technique used in AI and data analysis to estimate data points between known data points, often used for smoothing and curve fitting.

Intrinsic Reward: A reward signal generated within an AI system, often used in reinforcement learning to encourage certain behaviors or exploration.

Invariance: Property of AI models remaining consistent despite changes in input, such as rotation or scale.

Inverse Kinematics: In AI robotics, the process of determining the joint configurations of a robot to achieve a desired end-effector position or pose.

Inverse Reinforcement Learning: AI approach where agents learn task rewards by observing expert behavior.

Iterative Refinement: A process in AI and optimization where a solution is repeatedly improved through a series of iterations or refinements.

J

Jaccard Distance: A metric used in AI to measure the dissimilarity between two sets, often used in clustering and recommendation systems.

Jaccard Index: Evaluation metric used to measure the similarity between two sets in AI tasks.

Java AI Libraries: Libraries and frameworks in the Java programming language that facilitate AI and machine learning development.

Job Scheduling: The process of assigning tasks or jobs to computing resources in an efficient manner, often used in AI clusters and data centers.

Joint Learning: A machine learning approach where multiple AI models are trained together to solve a common task, often leading to improved performance.

Joint Probability Distribution: AI concept representing the probabilities of multiple random variables occurring together.

JSON (JavaScript Object Notation): A lightweight data interchange format often used in AI for data serialization and communication between systems.

Jupyter Notebook: An interactive coding environment often used for AI development and data analysis.

K

Kernel Methods: Techniques for transforming data into a higher-dimensional space to simplify complex relationships.

Kernel PCA (Principal Component Analysis): A dimensionality reduction technique in AI that uses kernel methods to map data into a higher-dimensional space for PCA.

Kernel Trick: Technique to implicitly map data into higher-dimensional spaces, often used in SVMs.

Keyword Extraction: An AI natural language processing task that involves identifying and extracting important words or phrases from text documents.

Keyword Spotting: An AI speech recognition task that involves identifying and recognizing specific keywords or phrases in spoken language.

K-Means Clustering: Popular AI algorithm for partitioning data into clusters based on similarity.

K-Nearest Neighbors (KNN): A machine learning algorithm that classifies data points based on the majority class among their k-nearest neighbors in a feature space.

Knowledge Base: A repository of structured knowledge or information that AI systems can access and use for reasoning and problem-solving.

Knowledge Distillation: Technique where a large, complex AI model is trained to transfer its knowledge to a smaller model.

Knowledge Engineering: The process of creating knowledge bases, ontologies, and rule-based systems for AI applications, often used in expert systems.

Knowledge Extraction: The process of automatically extracting structured information or facts from unstructured data sources, such as text or documents.

Knowledge Graphs: Graph-based AI structures representing relationships between entities, aiding in semantic understanding.

Knowledge Representation: The process of encoding knowledge, information, or data in a structured format that AI systems can use for reasoning and decision-making.

Knowledge Transfer: The process of transferring knowledge or learned patterns from one AI model to another, often used to improve model performance.

Kullback-Leibler Divergence: Measure of the difference between two probability distributions in AI.

L

L2 Regularization: Technique to prevent overfitting in AI models by penalizing large parameter values.

Label Propagation: A semi-supervised learning technique in AI where labels from labeled data points are propagated to neighboring unlabeled data points in a graph.

Label Smoothing: A regularization technique in AI where the model is penalized for assigning high confidence to correct labels, promoting robustness.

Language Modeling: An AI task where models generate coherent and contextually relevant text, often used in natural language processing tasks like text generation and machine translation.

Large Language Model (LLM): AI model trained on extensive text data to understand and generate human-like language.

Latent Dirichlet Allocation (LDA): A probabilistic topic modeling technique in AI used for discovering topics within a collection of documents.

Latent Space: Low-dimensional representation of data learned by AI models, useful for visualization and manipulation.

Layer Normalization: A technique in deep learning to normalize the activations of neurons within a neural network layer, improving training stability.

Leaky ReLU (Rectified Linear Unit): An activation function in neural networks that allows a small, non-zero gradient for negative inputs, preventing the "dying ReLU" problem.

Learning Rate: A hyperparameter in AI optimization algorithms that determines the step size during model parameter updates.

Lifelong Learning: Continual learning over long timescales.

Linear Regression: Basic AI technique for modeling the relationship between a dependent variable and independent variables.

Link Analysis: An AI technique that examines the relationships or links between entities in a network, often used in social network analysis and search engine algorithms.

Link Prediction: An AI task involving the prediction of missing or future links in a network or graph.

Local Minima: Points in AI optimization where loss functions have lower values, but may not be the global minimum.

Local Search: An optimization technique in AI that explores the search space by iteratively improving solutions from a local neighborhood.

Logical AI: Using logic representations and reasoning in AI.

Logistic Regression: An AI modeling technique used for binary classification problems, estimating the probability of an instance belonging to a particular class.

Long Short-Term Memory (LSTM): A type of recurrent neural network architecture suitable for processing sequences.

Long-Tail Distribution: Distribution where a large number of categories have relatively few occurrences, common in real-world data.

Long-Term Memory (LTM): Enabling neural networks to remember previously learned information.

Loss Function: A mathematical measure used to quantify the difference between predicted and actual values in AI training.

Low-Level Features: Basic and primitive features or characteristics of data, often used in computer vision and signal processing.

M

Machine Learning (ML): AI component enabling computers to learn and predict outcomes without explicit programming.

Machine Translation: The task of automatically translating text or speech from one language to another using AI and natural language processing.

Manifold Learning: Techniques in AI and machine learning used to discover and visualize the underlying structure or manifold in high-dimensional data.

Market Basket Analysis: An AI data mining technique that identifies patterns and relationships between products frequently purchased together in retail transactions.

Markov Chain Monte Carlo (MCMC): Computational technique used in AI for sampling complex probability distributions.

Markov Decision Process (MDP): A mathematical framework in AI used for modeling decision-making in situations with uncertainty and sequential actions.

Maximum Likelihood Estimation (MLE): A statistical method used in AI to estimate the parameters of a model that maximizes the likelihood of observed data.

Memory Networks: AI architectures designed to store and retrieve information for better contextual understanding.

Metaheuristic Algorithms: Optimization algorithms in AI that are used to find approximate solutions to complex problems, often inspired by natural processes.

Meta-Learning: An AI approach where models are trained to learn how to learn, enabling them to adapt quickly to new tasks or domains.

Microservices: A software architectural style where an application is divided into small, independently deployable services, often used in AI systems.

Microsoft Bing: Microsoft's search engine using AI for results, akin to Google Bard, with internet connectivity.

Mixed-Integer Programming: An optimization technique in AI that deals with linear programming problems where some variables are constrained to be integers.

Mobile AI: AI models and applications designed to run efficiently on mobile devices, such as smartphones and tablets.

Model Compression: Reducing model size while retaining performance.

Model Distillation: Transferring model knowledge from larger to smaller models.

Model Quantization: Reducing numerical precision of weights to save memory.

Model Validation: Process of assessing an AI model's performance and generalization on unseen data.

Model-Based Reinforcement Learning: A category of reinforcement learning where agents build a model of the environment to make decisions.

Model-Free Methods: Techniques in AI where models are not explicitly created to make predictions or decisions, often used in reinforcement learning.

Model-Free Reinforcement Learning: A category of reinforcement learning where agents learn to make decisions without explicitly modeling the environment.

Modular Architecture: Dividing complex models into simpler interconnected sub-models.

Moral AI: The study of ethical and moral considerations in the development and deployment of AI systems.

Multi-Agent Reinforcement Learning: Training multiple interacting agents using RL.

Multiclass Classification: AI task of assigning a single label to an input from multiple possible categories.

Multi-Instance Learning: An AI approach where data is organized into bags, and the goal is to classify bags based on the presence of positive instances.

Multilabel Classification: AI task of assigning multiple labels to a single input, useful for complex categorization.

Multilayer Perceptron: Neural network architecture with multiple layers between input and output layers.

Multimodal AI: AI processing various inputs, including text, images, videos, and speech.

Multi-Modal Learning: AI approach that combines information from different data modalities, like text and images.

Multi-Objective Learning: Optimizing for multiple objectives simultaneously in machine learning.

Multi-Task Learning: Jointly training model on multiple objectives and datasets.

N

Natural Language Generation (NLG): AI process of producing human-like language from data.

Natural Language Interface: An AI interface that allows users to interact with computers using natural language, often used in chatbots and virtual assistants.

Natural Language Processing: AI branch using machine learning to enable computers to understand human language.

Natural Language Query: An AI query that allows users to ask questions in human language to retrieve information from databases or knowledge bases.

Natural Language Understanding (NLU): AI's ability to comprehend and derive meaning from human language.

Negative Sampling: A technique in AI for training models, often used in recommendation systems, where negative examples are sampled to balance the training dataset.

Network Pruning: A technique in AI model optimization where redundant or less important connections in neural networks are removed to reduce model size.

Neural Architecture Search: AI process of automating the design of neural network architectures.

Neural Network: Computational model emulating the human brain's pattern recognition, consisting of interconnected neurons.

Neural ODE (Ordinary Differential Equation): An AI modeling technique that represents neural networks as continuous dynamical systems described by differential equations.

Neural Style Transfer: Technique using AI to apply the artistic style of one image to the content of another.

Neuroethics: The study of ethical considerations related to the development and use of AI systems inspired by the human brain.

Neuroevolution: A type of AI optimization where artificial neural networks are evolved through genetic algorithms or other evolutionary strategies.

Neuromorphic Computing: A computing paradigm inspired by the structure and function of the human brain, often used for AI applications.

Neuromorphic Hardware: Specialized hardware designed to mimic the structure and operation of the human brain, often used for AI tasks requiring low power consumption and high efficiency.

Neurosymbolic AI: An approach that combines neural networks and symbolic reasoning in AI systems to enhance understanding and problem-solving.

No-Free-Lunch Theorem: A theorem in AI and optimization that states there is no universal optimization algorithm that works best for all problems.

Noise Injection: Adding controlled noise to data in AI models to improve generalization.

Nonparametric Models: AI models that do not make strong assumptions about the functional form of the data distribution, often used in density estimation and clustering.

Normalization: Process of scaling input data to a standard range to improve AI model training.

Normalizing Flows: AI models used for density estimation and generative tasks by transforming simple distributions into complex ones.

O

Object Detection: AI task of identifying and locating specific objects within images or videos.

Object Localization: An AI task that involves not only detecting objects within images or videos but also precisely identifying their locations or boundaries.

Object Recognition: AI task of identifying objects within images or videos, often involving multiple categories.

Objective Function: In AI optimization, it's a mathematical function used to measure the performance or quality of a model, which is typically minimized or maximized during training.

One-Shot Learning: AI task where models are trained on a single example per class.

Online Learning: A machine learning approach where AI models are updated continuously as new data becomes available, allowing them to adapt to changing environments.

Online Recommender System: An AI system that provides real-time recommendations to users based on their current behavior and preferences.

Ontology Engineering: The process of creating and maintaining ontologies, which define concepts, relationships, and taxonomies within a specific domain for AI applications.

Ontology: Specifying concepts and relationships in a domain using formal logic semantics.

OpenAI: A prominent AI research organization known for its contributions to the field of artificial intelligence and machine learning.

Optical Character Recognition (OCR): Identifying text content in images.

Optical Flow: An AI computer vision technique that estimates the motion of objects in a video sequence by analyzing the apparent motion of pixels between frames.

Optimization Algorithm: A method in AI for finding the best solution or parameter values that minimize or maximize an objective function.

Ordinal Regression: An AI technique for predicting ordinal variables or ordered categories, often used when the dependent variable has a natural order.

Outlier Detection: AI task of identifying data points that deviate significantly from the norm.

Overfitting: AI model learning training data too well, performing poorly on new, unseen data.

Overlapping Clustering: An AI clustering technique where data points can belong to multiple clusters simultaneously, often used in fuzzy clustering.

P

Parallel Computing: The use of multiple processors or computing units to perform AI tasks simultaneously, often used to speed up model training and complex computations.

Parameters: Numerical values influencing AI structure and behavior.

Pareto Optimization: An AI optimization technique that aims to find solutions that are optimal with respect to multiple conflicting objectives, without worsening any one objective.

Pattern Recognition: The process in AI of identifying and classifying patterns within data, often used in image recognition and speech recognition.

Peer-to-Peer (P2P) Networks: A decentralized network architecture in AI and computing where participants communicate and share resources directly with one another, often used in file sharing and distributed systems.

Perceptron: Basic building block of neural networks, simulating the function of a single neuron.

Permutation Testing: An AI statistical method that assesses the significance of an observed effect by randomly permuting the data and comparing it to the actual results.

Personalization: An AI strategy that tailors content, recommendations, or experiences to individual users based on their preferences and behavior.

Poisson Distribution: A probability distribution often used in AI and statistics to model the number of events occurring in a fixed interval of time or space.

Policy Gradient Methods: A class of reinforcement learning algorithms that directly optimize the policy of an agent by adjusting its parameters.

Precision and Recall: Evaluation metrics measuring the accuracy and completeness of AI model predictions.

Predictive Modeling: The use of AI and statistical techniques to make predictions or forecasts based on historical data and patterns.

Pretrained Model: An AI model that has been trained on a large dataset for a specific task and can be fine-tuned for a related task with less data.

Principal Component Analysis (PCA): AI technique to reduce dimensionality in data by finding orthogonal linear combinations of variables.

Principle of Least Privilege: A security principle in AI and computer systems that restricts access rights to only those necessary for a user or process to perform their tasks.

Probabilistic Graphical Models: AI models that use graphical representations to encode and reason about probabilistic relationships between variables, including Bayesian networks and Markov random fields.

Probabilistic Programming: An AI programming paradigm that incorporates uncertainty and probability into algorithms and models, often used in Bayesian inference.

Procedural Content Generation: Algorithmically generating game levels, textures, music, stories, etc.

Pruning: Technique involving the removal of unnecessary connections or neurons in a neural network to enhance efficiency.

Public Key Infrastructure (PKI): A security framework in AI that uses public and private keys for secure communication and data protection.

Q

Quality Assurance (QA): In AI and software development, it refers to the process of ensuring the quality and reliability of AI models, software, or products through testing and validation.

Quality of Service (QoS): In AI and networking, it measures the level of service quality provided to users or applications, often involving metrics like latency and bandwidth.

Quantile: A statistical measure in AI and data analysis that represents a specific point in a data distribution, often used to summarize data or calculate percentiles.

Quantization: In AI and signal processing, it refers to the process of reducing the number of distinct values in a dataset or model, often used to save memory or storage.

Quantum Computing: Computing using quantum bits (qubits) to perform complex calculations, potentially revolutionizing AI.

Quantum Entanglement: A quantum physics phenomenon where two or more particles become correlated in such a way that the state of one particle is dependent on the state of another, even when they are separated by great distances.

Quantum Machine Learning: Integration of quantum computing techniques with machine learning algorithms.

Quantum Supremacy: A concept in quantum computing referring to the point at which a quantum computer can perform tasks beyond the capabilities of classical computers.

Query Expansion: An AI information retrieval technique that broadens a search query to retrieve more relevant results by including synonyms, related terms, or variations.

Query Intent: An AI understanding of the underlying goal or purpose of a user's search query, often used to provide more relevant search results or recommendations.

Query Language: A specialized language in AI and databases used to retrieve and manipulate data from a database, often used in SQL (Structured Query Language).

Query Optimization: An AI database management technique that improves the efficiency of database queries by selecting the most efficient query execution plan.

Queue Management: An AI technique for optimizing the allocation and processing of tasks or requests in a queue, often used in resource scheduling and service systems.

Quick Sort: Sorting algorithm used in AI and computer science to efficiently order elements in a list.

R

Radial Basis Function (RBF): A type of artificial neural network activation function used in machine learning and pattern recognition.

Random Forest: Ensemble learning method that constructs multiple decision trees to improve prediction accuracy.

Random Search: An AI optimization technique that explores hyperparameter configurations randomly rather than using a systematic search strategy.

Recommender System: An AI application that provides personalized recommendations to users, often used in e-commerce and content recommendation.

Recurrent Neural Network (RNN): Neural network architecture designed to process sequences of data by incorporating previous outputs.

Recurrent Reinforcement Learning: An AI approach that combines recurrent neural networks with reinforcement learning for tasks involving sequential data.

Recurrent Reinforcement Learning: An AI approach that combines recurrent neural networks with reinforcement learning for tasks involving sequential data.

Redundancy: In AI and data storage, it refers to the duplication of data or components to improve reliability and fault tolerance.

Regression Analysis: AI technique used to predict continuous numerical values based on input variables.

Regression Trees: A machine learning model that uses decision trees to perform regression, predicting numerical values based on input features.

Regularization: Techniques to prevent overfitting in AI models by adding a penalty term to the loss function.

Reinforcement Learning: AI learning method where agents learn through interactions with an environment and rewards.

Reinforcement Learning: Learning paradigm where agents make decisions to maximize rewards in an environment.

Reinforcement Signal: In reinforcement learning, it represents the feedback or reward signal provided to an agent based on its actions in an environment.

Reinforcement Signal: In reinforcement learning, it represents the feedback or reward signal provided to an agent based on its actions in an environment.

Residual Network (ResNet): A type of deep neural network architecture designed to address the vanishing gradient problem in deep learning.

Risk Assessment: An AI process of evaluating potential risks and their impact in various scenarios, often used in risk management and decision-making.

Robotic Process Automation (RPA): The use of software robots to automate repetitive tasks in business processes.

Robotic Vision: The use of computer vision and AI in robotics to enable robots to perceive and interact with their environment.

Robustness Testing: Evaluating AI models under various conditions to assess their resilience and reliability.

Rule-Based System: An AI system that uses a set of predefined rules and logic to make decisions or perform tasks, often used in expert systems.

S

Self-Attention: Mechanism within AI models that focuses on different parts of input data to weigh their importance.

Self-Driving Cars: Autonomous vehicles equipped with AI systems that can navigate and operate without human intervention.

Self-Organizing Maps (SOM): AI models that use unsupervised learning to map high-dimensional data into a lower-dimensional representation, often used for clustering and visualization.

Self-Similarity: Property where a data element is similar to a subset of itself, often used in pattern recognition.

Self-Supervised Learning: AI learning method where models generate labels from input data to facilitate training.

Self-Taught Learning: An AI learning paradigm where models are trained on a large dataset without explicit labels and then fine-tuned on a smaller labeled dataset.

Semantic Analysis: An AI process of extracting and understanding the meaning and context of text or data.

Semantic Search: AI approach for understanding the meaning behind user queries to deliver relevant search results.

Semantic Segmentation: AI task of classifying and labeling each pixel in an image, enabling detailed object identification.

Semi-Supervised Learning: Learning paradigm using a combination of labeled and unlabeled data for training.

Sentiment Analysis: AI task of determining the emotional tone or attitude expressed in text.

Sentiment Classification: An AI task of categorizing text or opinions into positive, negative, or neutral sentiments.

Sequence-to-Sequence Models: AI architecture that takes sequences as input and produces sequences as output, useful for tasks like machine translation.

Simulated Annealing: An AI optimization algorithm inspired by annealing in metallurgy, often used to find global optima in complex search spaces.

Spam Filter: An AI application that uses machine learning to detect and filter out unwanted or spam emails.

Sparse Coding: An AI technique that represents data as a combination of a small number of basis functions, often used in feature learning and dimensionality reduction.

Spectral Clustering: An AI clustering technique that uses spectral graph theory to partition data into clusters based on similarities in a graph representation.

Stacking: Ensemble learning method that combines predictions from multiple AI models.

Statistical Learning Theory: A field in AI and machine learning that focuses on understanding the theoretical foundations and properties of learning algorithms.

Stochastic Parrot: Analogy illustrating AI's lack of deep understanding, akin to a parrot mimicking speech.

Style Transfer: Adapting one image's style to another's content, allowing AI to generate novel visual attributes.

Superintelligence: A hypothetical AI system that possesses intelligence surpassing human capabilities across a wide range of tasks.

Supervised Learning: A machine learning paradigm where AI models are trained on labeled data to make predictions or classifications.

Support Vector Machine (SVM): AI algorithm for classification and regression tasks, maximizing the margin between classes.

Swarm Intelligence: An AI approach inspired by the collective behavior of social insects, where multiple agents interact to solve complex problems.

Synthetic Data: Artificially generated data used for training AI models when real data is limited or sensitive.

Synthetic Voice Generation: AI-driven technology creating human-like speech from text inputs.

T

Target Variable: In supervised learning, it's the variable that AI models aim to predict or classify based on input features.

Temporal Difference Learning: Reinforcement learning approach where agents learn through temporal differences in rewards.

Temperature: Parameters controlling randomness in language model outputs.

Temporal Convolutional Network (TCN): A type of neural network architecture designed for sequential data processing, such as time series analysis.

Text Classification: AI task of categorizing text documents into predefined classes or categories.

Text-to-Image Generation: Creating images based on textual descriptions.

Time Complexity: A measure in AI and computer science that quantifies the computational resources required to solve a problem as a function of input size.

Time Series Analysis: AI approach for analyzing data points ordered over time, often used in forecasting.

Time Series Forecasting: AI task of predicting future data points based on past observations in sequential data.

Top-k Sampling: An AI text generation technique that selects the top-k most likely next tokens to reduce randomness in generated text.

Training Data: Datasets used to educate AI models.

Transduction: The process of mapping input data to output data in AI tasks.

Transfer Learning: Leveraging pre-trained AI models to enhance performance on a new, related task.

Transferability: The extent to which knowledge gained from one task can be applied to improve performance on another task.

Transformative AI: AI systems that have the potential to significantly transform industries, societies, or human activities.

Transformer Architecture: Deep learning architecture processing context in data relationships.

Transformer Model: Deep learning architecture processing context in data relationships.

Transformers (Attention): Neural network architecture using attention mechanism, effective for sequences.

Transparency: The degree to which AI models' decisions and actions are understandable and interpretable by humans.

Trustworthiness: The reliability and credibility of AI systems in making predictions or decisions, often associated with ethical AI design.

U

Uncertainty Estimation: The process of quantifying and representing the uncertainty associated with AI model predictions or decisions.

Underfitting: A situation in AI modeling where a model is too simple to capture the underlying patterns in the data, leading to poor performance.

Universal Approximation Theorem: A mathematical theorem in AI and neural networks that states that neural networks can approximate any continuous function with sufficient complexity.

Unstructured Data: Data that lacks a specific, predefined format or organization, often requiring AI techniques for analysis.

Unsupervised Learning: A machine learning paradigm where AI models are trained on unlabeled data to find patterns and structures without explicit supervision.

User Experience (UX) Design: The process of designing AI systems and interfaces to optimize user satisfaction and usability.

User Interface (UI): The visual and interactive elements of AI applications that users interact with to communicate with the system.

Utility Function: In AI and decision theory, it represents a measure of the desirability or value of different outcomes or states.

V

Validation Set: A subset of data used during AI model development and training to evaluate its performance and tune hyperparameters.

Variance: Measure of the spread between data points, indicating the AI model's sensitivity to input changes.

Variational Autoencoder (VAE): A type of autoencoder in deep learning that is used for generative modeling and representation learning that learns a probabilistic mapping between data and a latent space.

Variational Inference: Technique for approximating complex probability distributions in AI models.

Vectorization: The process of converting data or operations into vector or matrix form for efficient computation in AI.

Virtual Reality (VR): Technology that uses AI and immersive experiences to simulate a virtual environment.

Voice Assistant: AI-powered software that responds to voice commands and performs tasks or provides information.

Voice Recognition: The AI task of converting spoken language into text, often used in voice assistants and transcription services.

Voice Synthesis: The AI process of generating human-like speech from text inputs, often used in virtual assistants and accessibility tools.

Voting Ensemble: An AI ensemble technique where multiple models' predictions are combined to make a final decision, often used for classification tasks.

W

Weak AI (Narrow AI): Task-specific AI limited to its defined capabilities.

Weak Supervision: Training AI models using noisy, incomplete, or imprecise labels instead of fully annotated data.

Web Scraping: AI process of extracting data from websites for analysis or other purposes.

Weight Initialization: The process of setting initial values for weights in AI neural networks, affecting training and convergence.

White Box Model: AI model with transparent and interpretable internal workings, aiding understanding and accountability.

Word Embeddings: Numeric representations of words used by AI models to understand semantic relationships.

Word2Vec: A technique that represents words as numerical vectors based on their contextual usage in text.

X

XAI (Explainable Artificial Intelligence): An important aspect of AI and machine learning focused on making AI models and their decisions more transparent and understandable to humans. XAI techniques aim to provide explanations for AI predictions and actions, especially in critical applications where transparency and accountability are essential.

XGBoost: Popular gradient boosting AI algorithm used for regression and classification tasks.

X-Ray Vision: AI application using computer vision to analyze medical X-ray images for diagnostics.

Y

YAML (YAML Ain't Markup Language): A human-readable data serialization format used in AI and software development to configure and represent data structures.

YARN (Yet Another Resource Negotiator): A resource management and job scheduling component in the Hadoop ecosystem used for managing resources in big data processing, including AI workloads.

Yield Management: AI-driven pricing strategy often used in the hospitality and airline industries to maximize revenue by adjusting prices based on demand and inventory levels.

Yield Optimization: AI application in digital advertising and e-commerce that maximizes the return on investment by optimizing ad placements and product recommendations for each user.

Yottabyte (YB): A unit of digital information storage often used in discussions about big data and AI, equal to 1,024 zettabytes or 2^80 bytes.

You Only Look Once (YOLO): A popular real-time object detection system in computer vision that uses deep learning and convolutional neural networks (CNNs) to detect and locate objects in images and videos.

YouTube Algorithm: The AI-driven recommendation algorithm used by YouTube to suggest videos to users based on their viewing history and preferences. This algorithm plays a crucial role in content discovery on the platform.

Yule-Simon Distribution: A probability distribution used in statistical modeling and machine learning to describe data with heavy-tailed distributions, often applied in text analysis and natural language processing (NLP).

Yule-Walker Equations: A set of equations used in time series analysis and signal processing to estimate autoregressive model coefficients, a common technique in AI for modeling sequential data.

Z

Zero-Coupon Bond: AI application in finance modeling representing a bond that doesn't pay periodic interest.

Zero-Day Attack: Cyberattack exploiting a vulnerability in software before it's known and patched.

Zero-Day Vulnerability: A security flaw in software that hackers exploit before developers are aware of it.

Zero-Knowledge Proof: A cryptographic technique used in AI and security to prove that a statement is true without revealing any specific details about the statement itself.

Zero-Shot Learning: AI learning approach where models perform tasks without explicit training on those tasks.

Conclusion

Congratulations on completing your exploration of this glossary of AI terminology! You have now embarked on a journey to demystify the complex world of Artificial Intelligence. The vast array of terms, concepts, and methodologies you have encountered forms the foundation of this dynamic field. With this knowledge, you are better equipped to navigate discussions, engage in research, and contribute to the ever-evolving landscape of AI.

Remember that AI is not just a collection of technical terms, but a powerful force that shapes our society, industries, and daily lives. The definitions you have read in this glossary serve as gateways to beginning to understand the capabilities, challenges, and ethical considerations that come with harnessing AI's potential. Whether you are an academic, researcher, student, or enthusiast, this glossary empowers you to begin to engage confidently in AI conversations and explorations.

Further Reading & Sources

Your journey doesn't have to end here!

Delve deeper into the world of AI by exploring these recommended resources:

"Artificial Intelligence: A Modern Approach" by Stuart Russell and Peter Norvig - This comprehensive textbook offers a thorough introduction to the fundamentals of AI, covering a wide range of topics and concepts.

"Deep Learning" by Ian Goodfellow, Yoshua Bengio, and Aaron Courville - Dive into the realm of deep learning with this book, which provides insights into neural networks, optimization, and state-of-the-art techniques.

"Neural Networks and Deep Learning: A Textbook" by Charu C. Aggarwal: This book provides a detailed exploration of neural networks and their applications in deep learning, making it a valuable resource for those interested in this subfield.

"Reinforcement Learning: An Introduction" by Richard S. Sutton and Andrew G. Barto: If you're interested in reinforcement learning, this book is a comprehensive guide to the fundamentals and advanced concepts in the field.

"Superintelligence: Paths, Dangers, Strategies" by Nick Bostrom - Explore the implications of artificial general intelligence and the potential impact it could have on society.

"The AI Alignment Problem" by Brian Christian: Explore the critical challenge of aligning AI systems with human values and goals in this thought-provoking essay.

"The Hundred-Page Machine Learning Book" by Andriy Burkov - A concise guide to machine learning concepts and algorithms, perfect for both beginners and those seeking a refresher.

"AI: A Very Short Introduction" by Margaret A. Boden: For readers seeking a concise yet informative overview of AI's history, capabilities, and ethical implications, this book offers valuable insights.

"Ethics of Artificial Intelligence and Robotics" edited by Vincent C. Müller: As AI ethics is becoming increasingly important, this anthology compiles various perspectives on the ethical challenges posed by AI and robotics.

Online Courses - Platforms like Coursera, edX, and Khan Academy offer a variety of AI courses suitable for different skill levels, taught by experts in the field.

Research Papers and Journals - Engage with the latest research and advancements in AI by reading academic papers and journals from conferences like NeurIPS, ICML, and ACL.

AI Blogs and News Outlets - Stay up-to-date with AI trends, news, and insights by following blogs and websites like OpenAI, Towards Data Science, and AI Ethics.

AI Communities: Join online AI communities such as Reddit's r/Machine Learning and Stack Exchange's AI section to ask questions, share knowledge, and stay connected with the AI community.

AI Conferences and Workshops: Beyond reading research papers, consider attending AI conferences and workshops like NeurIPS, ICML, and ACL in person or virtually to engage with experts, discover emerging trends, and network with fellow enthusiasts.

AI Podcasts: Don't overlook the power of podcasts. Shows like "Artificial Intelligence with Lex Fridman," "Machine Learning Street Talk," and "Talking Machines" provide valuable insights and interviews with AI experts.

Remember, the world of AI is continuously evolving, and staying informed is essential to remain at the forefront of this dynamic field. Whether you're a student, a researcher, a practitioner, or simply curious, these resources will guide you on your journey to explore the limitless possibilities and challenges that AI brings to our world.

Dear Readers,

Please remember that the landscape of AI resources is continually evolving, and it's advisable for readers to explore the most up-to-date materials and communities to stay at the cutting edge of AI knowledge.

Free AI Tools & Resources

Free AI Services on the Internet

AI Chat: This is a chatbot that can be used to chat with AI researchers and developers.

AI Dungeon: This is a text-based adventure game that uses AI to generate the story. It is free to play.

AI Podcast: This is a podcast that interviews AI experts.

AI Today: This is a newsletter that covers the latest news about AI.

AIcrowd: This platform hosts a variety of AI competitions. You can participate in these competitions to learn about AI and to win prizes.

Amazon Web Services (AWS): This platform offers a variety of AI services, including machine learning, natural language processing, and computer vision. It is free to use for the first 12 months.

CaffeineAI: This is a tool that can be used to generate creative text formats, like poems, code, scripts, musical pieces, email, letters, etc. It is free to use for up to 1000 characters per month.

ChatGPT: This is a large language model that can be used to generate text, translate languages, and write different kinds of creative content. It is free to use for personal use.

DALL-E 2: This is a tool that can be used to generate images from text descriptions. It is still under development, but it is available for free to a limited number of users.

DALL-E Mini: This is a free online tool that uses AI to generate images from text descriptions.

DeepDream Generator: This is a tool that can be used to create psychedelic images using AI. It is free to use.

DeepL: This is a free online translator that uses AI to translate text between over 26 languages.

GANPaint: This is a tool that can be used to create images using AI. It is free to use.

GitHub: This is a code hosting platform where you can find and share AI projects.

Google AI Experiments: This website offers a variety of free AI experiments that you can try out. These experiments cover a wide range of topics, such as natural language processing, machine vision, and robotics.

Google AI Hub: This is a repository of AI datasets, tools, and resources. It is free to use.

Google AI Platform: This platform offers a variety of AI services, including machine learning, natural language processing, and computer vision. It is free to use for small projects.

Google Cloud AutoML Natural Language: This service allows you to train your own machine learning models for natural language processing tasks, such as sentiment analysis, text classification, and question answering. It is free to use for the first 10,000 text documents.

Google Cloud AutoML Translation: This service allows you to train your own machine learning models for machine translation. It is free to use for the first 10,000 translated words.

Google Cloud AutoML Vision: This service allows you to train your own machine learning models for image classification, object detection, and other tasks. It is free to use for the first 100,000 images.

Google Colab: This is a free online notebook environment that allows you to run Python code. It includes a variety of AI libraries, so you can use it to experiment with AI without having to install any software.

Grammarly: This is a tool that can be used to check grammar and spelling. It is free to use for basic features.

Hemingway Editor: This is a tool that can be used to improve the readability of your writing. It is free to use.

Hugging Face: This is a community platform for sharing and using AI models. It includes a variety of pre-trained models that you can use for free.

IBM Watson: This platform offers a variety of AI services, including natural language processing, machine translation, and image recognition. It is free to use for non-commercial projects.

Imagen: This is a tool that can be used to create images from text descriptions. It is free to use.

Imgur Upscaler: This is a free online tool that uses AI to upscale images.

Jarvis AI: This is a chatbot platform that allows you to create chatbots for your website or app. It is free to use for up to 1000 conversations per month.

Kaggle: This platform is similar to AIcrowd. It hosts a variety of AI competitions and datasets.

LaMDA: This is a large language model from Google AI that can be used for a variety of tasks, such as generating text, translating languages, and writing different kinds of creative content. It is still under development, but it is available for free to researchers.

Microsoft Azure AI: This platform offers a similar set of AI services to Google AI Platform. It is also free to use for small projects.

OpenAI API Explorer: This is a tool that allows you to explore OpenAI's API. It is free to use.

OpenAI API: This API allows you to access OpenAI's GPT-3 language model. GPT-3 is a powerful language model that can be used for a variety of tasks, such as generating text, translating languages, and writing different kinds of creative content.

OpenAI Gym: This is a toolkit for reinforcement learning. It provides a variety of environments that you can use to train your reinforcement learning agents.

Papers With Code: This is a website that lists papers that have been implemented in code. It is a great resource for finding AI projects that you can use or contribute to.

Playground.tensorflow.org: This website allows you to experiment with TensorFlow, an open-source machine learning library. It is a great way to learn about TensorFlow and to create your own AI applications.

ProWritingAid: This is a tool that can be used to check grammar, spelling, and style. It is free to use for basic features.

Rephrase.ai: This is a tool that can be used to rephrase text. It is free to use for up to 500 words per month.

Stack Overflow: This is a question-and-answer forum where you can ask questions about AI.

Talk to Transformer: This is a chatbot that can be used to chat with a large language model. It is free to use.

Teachable Machine: This website allows you to create your own machine learning models without any coding experience. It is a great way to learn about machine learning and to create your own AI applications.

Unity ML-Agents: This is a toolkit for developing and training AI agents for games. It provides a variety of game environments and tools.

VQGAN-CLIP Text-to-Image: This is a tool that can be used to create images from text descriptions. It is free to use.

Wolfram Alpha: This is a knowledge engine that can answer your questions in a variety of ways, including text, images, and graphs. It is free to use for basic questions.

Wordtune: This is a tool that can be used to improve the clarity and conciseness of your writing. It is free to use for up to 1000 words per month.

Farewell

Dear Readers,

As we reach the final page of "Navigating AI Language: A Glossary Guide to Artificial Intelligence," I want to extend my deepest gratitude for embarking on this journey into the world of AI with me. It has been my privilege to be your guide through the complex and fascinating terrain of artificial intelligence.

I hope this book has not only clarified the often-bewildering terminology of AI but also ignited your curiosity and passion for this transformative field. AI is not just a topic of study; it is a journey of discovery, an exploration of possibilities that will shape our collective future.

My goal is to make AI understandable to everyone, whether you're new to the field, an experienced professional, or simply curious about the ways AI is changing our world. With each page you've turned, we hope you've found answers, gained insights, and discovered the limitless potential and challenges AI presents.

Remember that AI is a dynamic field, one that evolves daily. New technologies, breakthroughs, and ethical questions arise constantly. I encourage you to continue your exploration, to seek out the latest research, to engage with experts, and to share your knowledge with others.

I want to leave you with a message that is not just a farewell, but an invitation. I invite you to stay curious, stay informed, and stay inspired by the possibilities that AI holds. As you explore the ever-expanding landscape of AI, I hope that you will find the answers you seek, the solutions you dream of, and the innovations that will help to shape our future for the better.

Thank you for choosing "Navigating AI Language" as your companion on this journey. Your curiosity and dedication to understanding AI are what drive progress in this field. As I bid you farewell, I do so with immense gratitude and hope that our paths will cross again in the wondrous world of artificial intelligence.

With warm regards,

J. Ippolito

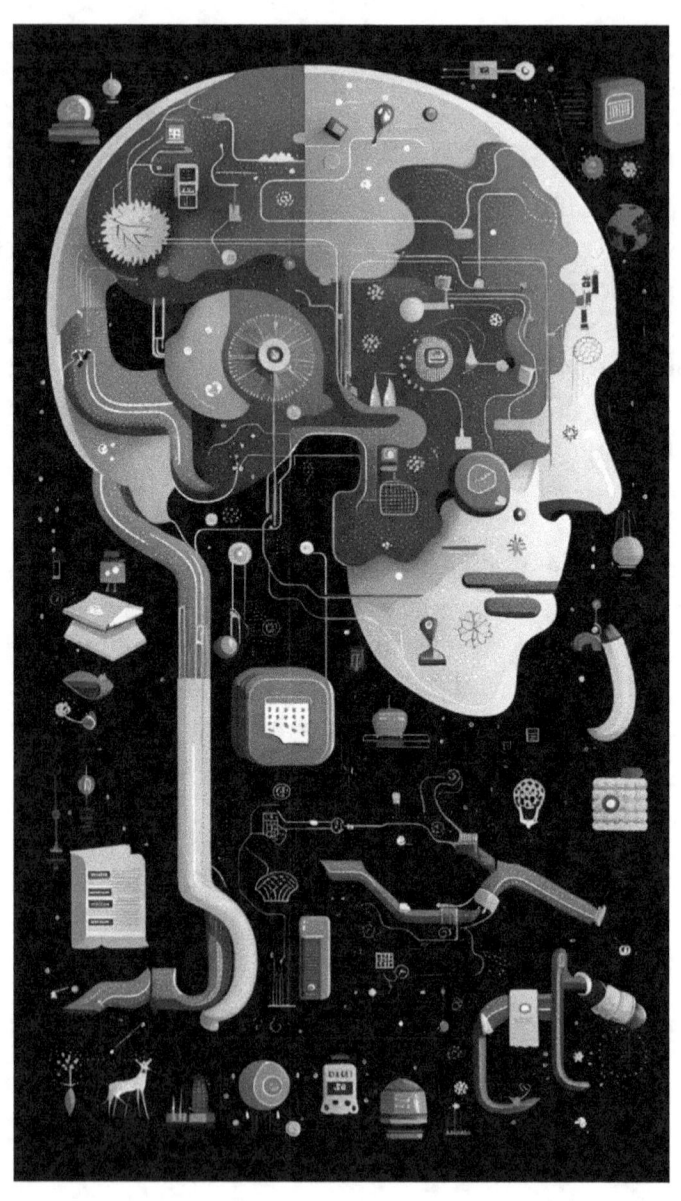

"The future has etched its indelible mark on our reality."